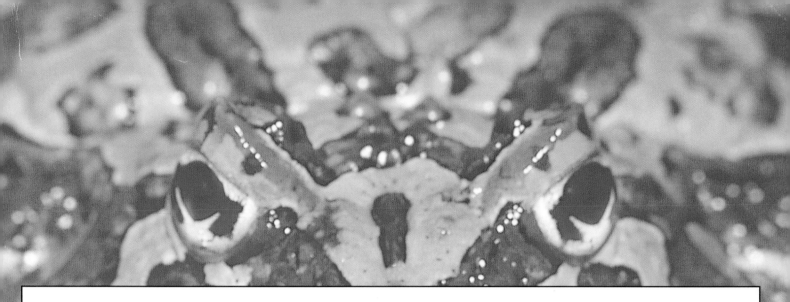

ANIMAL KINGDOM CLASSIFICATION

TREE FROGS, MUD PUPPIES & OTHER
AMPHIBIANS

By Daniel Gilpin
Content Adviser: Harold K. Voris, Ph.D., Curator and
Head, Division of Amphibians and Reptiles, Field Museum of
Natural History, Chicago

Science Adviser: Terrence E. Young Jr., M.Ed., M.L.S.,
Jefferson Parish (Louisiana) Public School System

First published in the United States in 2006 by
Compass Point Books
3109 West 50th St., #115
Minneapolis, MN 55410

ANIMAL KINGDOM CLASSIFICATION–AMPHIBIANS
was produced by

David West Children's Books
7 Princeton Court
55 Felsham Road
London SW15 1AZ

Copyright © 2005 David West Children's Books

Designer: David West
Editors: Gail Bushnell, Nadia Higgins
Page Production: Les Tranby, James Mackey

Visit Compass Point Books on the Internet at
www.compasspointbooks.com
or e-mail your request to
custserv@compasspointbooks.com

Library of Congress Cataloging-in-Publication Data
Gilpin, Daniel.
  Tree frogs, mud puppies & other amphibians /
  by Daniel Gilpin.
    p. cm.—(Animal kingdom classification)
  Includes bibliographical references and index.
  ISBN 0-7565-1249-2 (hardcover)
  1. Amphibians–Juvenile literature. I. Title. II. Series.
  QL644.2.G56 2006
  597.8—dc22   2005003683

PHOTO CREDITS:
Abbreviations: t-top, m-middle, b-bottom, r-right,
l-left, c-center.

Pages 8b, Martin Smith; 9tl, Oxford Scientific, 9tr, Jose B, Ruiz / naturepl.com; 11r, Doug Wechsler / naturepl.com; 13r, John Cancalosi / naturepl.com; 14b, Peter Oxford / naturepl.com; 15r, Suzannah Skelton, 15l, Paulo De Oliveira / Oxford Scientific, 15b, Benoit Beauregard; 16t, / naturepl.com; 16l & r, Barry Mansell / naturepl.com; 17l, Nicola brown, 17b, Ingo Arndt / naturepl.com; 18t, Michael Leach / Oxford Scientific; 19t, Michael Fogden / Oxford Scientific, 19l, Hans Christoph Kappel / naturepl.com; 20t, Kathie Atkinson / Oxford Scientific, 20b, Satoshi Kuribayashi / Oxford Scientific; 21t, Doug Wechsler / naturepl.com, 21l, Dodd, Kenneth Jr. / U.S. Fish and Wildlife Service; 22t, John Brown / Oxford Scientific, 22c, U.S. Fish and Wildlife Service, 22b, Fabrio Liverani / naturepl.com; 23t, Philip J. DeVries / Oxford Scientific, 23r, Doug Wechsler / naturepl.com, 23l, Jurgen Freund / naturepl.com; 24t, Hans Christoph Kappel / naturepl.com, 24b, Michael Fogden / Oxford Scientific; 25l, David Shale, naturepl.com, 25r, Philip Sharpe / Oxford Scientific, 25b, Phil Savoie / naturepl.com; 26c, Adrian Davis / naturepl.com, 26t, London Scientific Films / Oxford Scientific, 26b, Geoff Dore / naturepl.com; 27t, Tom Walmsley / naturepl.com, 27b, David M. Dennis / Oxford Scientific; 28t, 28l, Barry Mansell / naturepl.com, 28r, Michael Fogden / Oxford Scientific; 29l, Hans Christoph Kappel / naturepl.com, 29r, Doug Wechsler / naturepl.com; 30t, Tom Walmsley / naturepl.com, 30b, Laurie Knight; 31t, David H Coder, 31l, Paul Hobson / naturepl.com; page 33t, Terry McGleish; 34t, Jennings, Mark R. / U.S. Fish and Wildlife Service, 34c, Paul Baleta, 34l, Nick Garbutt / naturepl.com; 35t, Bruce Davidson / naturepl.com, 35l, David Curl / naturepl.com, 35r, Barry Mansell / naturepl.com; page 36t, Matthias Bandemer, 36l, Andrea Gingerich, 36b, Charles H. Smith / U.S. Fish and Wildlife Service; 37l, Barry Mansell / naturepl.com, 37r, Nick Garbutt / naturepl.com, 37b; 38b, Mark Payne-Gill / naturepl.com; page 39l, Andew Murray / naturepl.com, 39r, Brian Kenney / Oxford Scientific; 40t, George McCarthy / naturepl.com, 40b, Fabrio Liverani / naturepl.com; 41t, Mark Payne-Gill / naturepl.com, 41l, David Welling / naturepl.com; 42t, Aflo / naturepl.com, 42c, Terry McGleish; 43l, Peter Oxford / naturepl.com; 45b, Digital Vision.

Every effort has been made to contact copyright holders of any material reproduced in this book. Any omissions will be rectified in subsequent printings if notice is given to the publishers.

Front cover: Red-eyed tree frog
Opposite: Californian newt

KINGDOM CLASSIFICATION

TREE FROGS, MUD PUPPIES & OTHER
AMPHIBIANS

Daniel Gilpin

COMPASS POINT BOOKS ✦ MINNEAPOLIS, MINNESOTA

TABLE OF CONTENTS

INTRODUCTION

Amphibians are creatures of both fresh water and land. As adults, the majority of amphibians spend most of their time on land, although they must return to water to breed. Most young amphibians live and breathe in water like fish. Their bodies have to change through a process called metamorphosis before they can leave the water and come onto land.

Scientists classify, or sort, animals into different groups based on their shared characteristics. The six main groups of animals, from the most general to the most specific, are: phylum, class, order, family, genus, and species. Amphibians make up their own class among animals.

Like mammals or reptiles, amphibians are vertebrates. Their bodies have a backbone with a long spinal cord. All adult amphibians are carnivores. Young amphibians, which start life as legless tadpoles, eat tiny water creatures or scrape algae from underwater rocks or plants.

IN DAMP, DARK PLACES

Most adult amphibians, such as this salamander, have moist, slimy skin. As a result, they are only able to live in damp places or in habitats where the air is humid. Salamanders spend more time on land than most other amphibians, but they avoid bright, direct sunlight. Most hunt at night and spend the day under rocks or fallen branches to avoid drying out.

RANGE OF AMPHIBIANS

Amphibians fall into three main groups: frogs and toads; caecilians; and newts and salamanders. Frogs and toads have much longer back legs than front legs. Caecilians have no legs at all, while newts and salamanders have legs that are a similar size.

Tree frog

WHEREVER THERE'S WATER

Most amphibians need water to reproduce, so most do not stray far from the nearest pool or stream. Frogs and newts in particular spend a lot of time in the water, even as adults. As a group, amphibians are more closely related to fish than to any other vertebrates. Like fish, their young can breathe underwater, as can some adult amphibians.

Bullfrog

LEGS AND TAILS

The easiest way to tell the main types of amphibians apart is to look at their legs and tails. Caecilians have no legs at all and look a bit like giant earthworms. Adult frogs and toads have legs but no tail. Most frogs move by hopping, while toads tend to walk. Newts and salamanders have both legs and tails. The main difference between them is that adult newts have webbed fins on their tails, and salamanders do not.

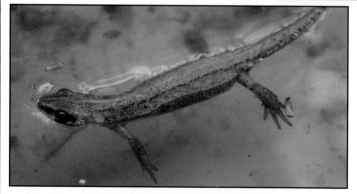

Newt

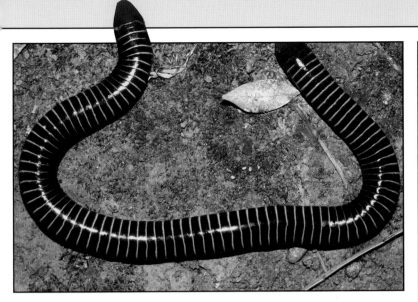

Caecilian

SHARP-RIBBED SALAMANDER

Unlike most salamanders, the sharp-ribbed salamander spends most of its life in water, which is why it is also sometimes called a newt. Its tail has a very short, narrow fin for swimming, and its ribs can be felt through the sides of its body. The position of its ribs is marked by bright orange bumps called tubercles. The sharp-ribbed salamander is relatively large, and adult males can grow up to 12 inches (30.5 centimeters) long.

The sharp-ribbed salamander lives in Spain, Portugal, and Morocco.

Toad

Salamander

9

AN AMPHIBIAN'S BODY

Most people have seen a frog at some point in their lives. These animals are probably the best known of all amphibians. All species of frog have soft, slimy skin and share the same basic body shape with four legs.

Cerebral hemisphere

Cerebellum

BRAIN
The brain controls the frog's behavior. The optic lobe processes vision, and the olfactory lobe controls taste and smell.

Olfactory lobe

Optic lobe

SPECIALIZED DESIGN
A frog's body is designed for life both in and out of water. Its back feet are webbed to help it swim, and its smooth body lets it glide easily through water. On land, a frog's front legs lift its head up off the ground, giving it a better view of its surroundings. The back legs are long and have powerful muscles to launch the frog into the air whenever it needs to hop.

Gall bladder

Tympanic membrane (eardrum)

Stomach

THREE-CHAMBERED HEART
Oxygen-rich blood from the lungs enters the left atrium. The right atrium, which wraps around the ventricle, receives deoxygenated blood from the rest of the body.

Left atrium

Right atrium

Spiral valve

IN AND OUT OF WATER
Frogs are equally at home in water or on land. In dry weather, they often return to water to keep their skin moist. They also need water to breed.

Ventricle

Testis   Nerve cord

Kidney

Except for a small area that
contains the brain, a frog's skull
is flat. The vertebral column is
made up of just nine bones and
houses the spinal cord, which
transmits nerve signals from the
body to the brain and back again.
Frogs have almost no neck and can
hardly move their heads.
The sacrum and urostyle form
the hips.

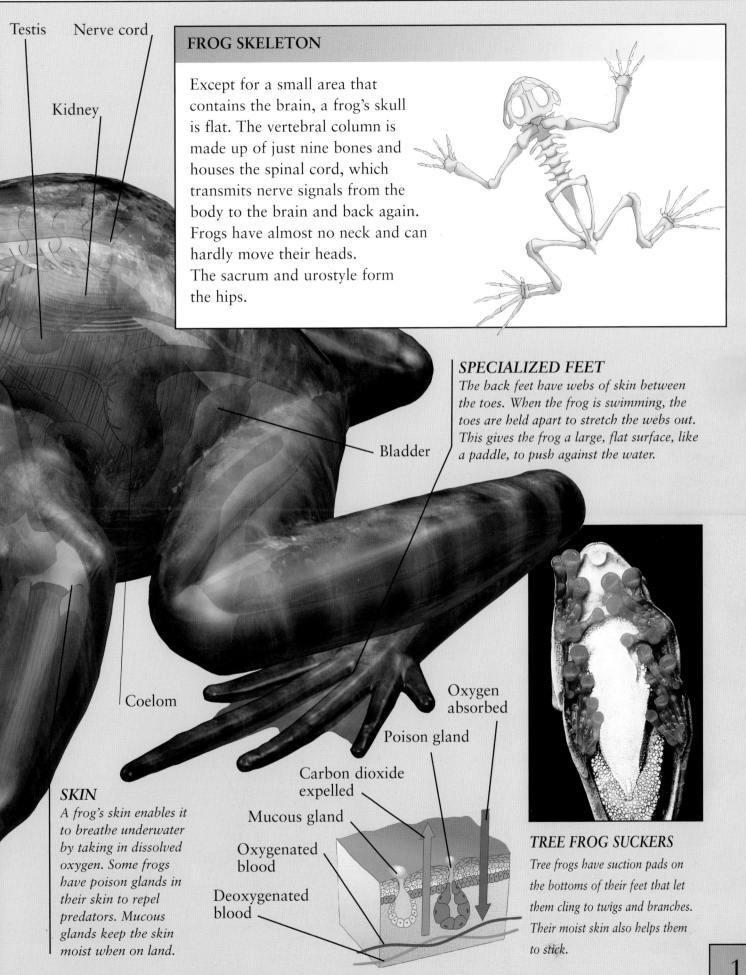

SPECIALIZED FEET

*The back feet have webs of skin between
the toes. When the frog is swimming, the
toes are held apart to stretch the webs out.
This gives the frog a large, flat surface, like
a paddle, to push against the water.*

Bladder

Coelom

Oxygen
absorbed

Poison gland

Carbon dioxide
expelled

Mucous gland

Oxygenated
blood

Deoxygenated
blood

SKIN

*A frog's skin enables it
to breathe underwater
by taking in dissolved
oxygen. Some frogs
have poison glands in
their skin to repel
predators. Mucous
glands keep the skin
moist when on land.*

TREE FROG SUCKERS

*Tree frogs have suction pads on
the bottoms of their feet that let
them cling to twigs and branches.
Their moist skin also helps them
to stick.*

11

ANCIENT AMPHIBIANS

Today's amphibians are tiny compared to some of their earliest ancestors. The predator *Mastodonsaurus* grew up to an amazing 13 feet (4 meters) long. It lived in the swamps of what is now Europe. Amphibians were the first vertebrates to come out of water and live on land.

FINS TO FEET

Amphibians evolved directly from fish. Their ancestors looked a bit like modern-day lungfish. They were able to breathe air and had fleshy fins full of small bones. Over millions of years, the fins of these fish slowly changed into legs and feet. These were first used to help the ancient amphibians move around on the beds of lakes and rivers. Over time, the legs became strong enough to pull the animals onto land. Being able to crawl on land gave amphibians an advantage. During droughts, they could leave shrinking pools and find more plentiful sources of water.

A NEW LIFE ON LAND

Eventually amphibians spent more time out of water than in it. Although there were no other land vertebrates in those days, there were plenty of invertebrates to hunt, including enormous millipedes and insects. Before the first reptiles evolved, amphibians ruled Earth.

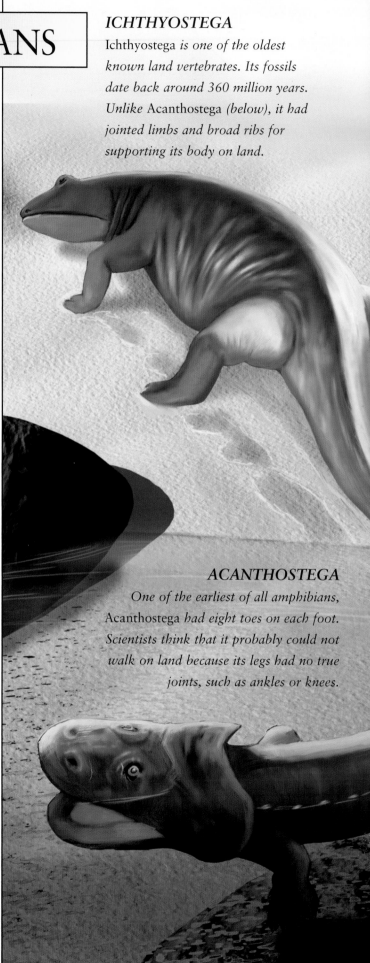

ICHTHYOSTEGA

Ichthyostega *is one of the oldest known land vertebrates. Its fossils date back around 360 million years. Unlike* Acanthostega *(below), it had jointed limbs and broad ribs for supporting its body on land.*

ACANTHOSTEGA

One of the earliest of all amphibians, Acanthostega *had eight toes on each foot. Scientists think that it probably could not walk on land because its legs had no true joints, such as ankles or knees.*

GERROTHORAX

Some ancient amphibians spent their whole lives in the water. *Gerrothorax* was one such animal. Instead of lungs for breathing air, it had feathery gills for removing oxygen from the water. Although it had four legs, its body was flattened and tadpolelike, even as an adult.

Gerrothorax grew up to 3 feet (90 cm) long.

FOSSIL EVIDENCE
The fossilized skeletons of frogs and other amphibians show scientists what they looked like.

EARLY FROGS

The first amphibians evolved more than 360 million years ago, but frogs and other modern amphibians did not appear until much later. The oldest frog fossils date from the Jurassic period, around 280 million years ago. By this time, Earth was home to many other land vertebrates, including dinosaurs and early mammals. Most of the giant amphibians had long since died out, although a few, such as *Koolasuchus*, still existed in small numbers.

SKIN AND SENSES

An amphibian's skin has two main jobs. It has to protect the body and help absorb oxygen. Amphibian senses are similar to our own, although their eyes and ears have important differences.

SKIN FOR BREATHING

Amphibians are unique in having skin that can take oxygen from the air. Vessels filled with low-oxygen blood run just underneath the skin and absorb the gas while releasing carbon dioxide. In this way, an amphibian's skin is a lot like a human lung. The main difference is that amphibians can also use their skin to remove oxygen from water.

WARTS AND ALL

Most amphibians have moist, slimy skin, but toads' skin is dry and covered with wartlike bumps. Having dry skin makes it easier for toads to survive long periods out of water. It also lets them live in drier habitats than those of frogs or other amphibians, although toads still have to return to fresh water to breed.

BIG, BAGGY SKIN

Lake Titicaca, in the Andes Mountains of South America, is one of the highest lakes in the world. It is also home to an extraordinary frog. Because it has such a high altitude, the lake and surrounding area are low in oxygen, both in the air and water. To combat this, the Lake Titicaca giant frog has huge folds of skin. The skin folds increase the area through which the frog can absorb oxygen.

The Lake Titicaca giant frog lives only in the lake after which it is named, high in the Andes Mountains between Peru and Bolivia.

EYES

Amphibian eyes are less sensitive than our own. Unlike the eyes of mammals, they are unable to change focus and see things clearly from a distance.

SIMPLE SENSES

Amphibians experience the world in less detail than we do. Their eyes and ears have a more simple structure, and their sense of smell is less developed, at least on land. Like us, amphibians have paired nostrils between their eyes and mouth, but they do not have the same long nasal passages.

MOUTH

The tongue is used more for catching prey than tasting it. Frogs and toads can curl their tongues around prey and pull it into their mouths.

EARS

The ears work on the same principle as human ears. However, in amphibians there is no outer ear structure. The eardrum is part of the skin and can be clearly seen behind the eye. There is just one bone in the middle ear, beneath the eardrum. In humans, there are three.

HIDING AND WARNING

Colors and patterns can help an amphibian hide from predators or tell them to leave it alone. Amphibians are some of the best camouflaged animals, as well as some of the most brightly colored.

The horned frog (bottom right of picture) is one of the best camouflaged amphibians. It has the perfect shape and color to blend in with leaves.

CAMOUFLAGE

One of the best ways to avoid being eaten is to stay out of sight. Some amphibians do this by hiding under logs or stones during the day and only coming out at night to feed. Others use camouflage to blend in with their surroundings. The colors and patterns on their skin match those of their habitat, making it harder for predators to see them. A few amphibians even copy, or mimic, the shapes of surrounding objects, such as fallen leaves.

COLOR-CHANGING TREE FROGS

Most amphibians have a fixed pattern and color, but some tree frogs can change their appearance. All frogs have special cells in their skin that contain pigments, the chemicals that give skin its color. The pigments are affected by the release of hormones in the blood. The pigments are moved inside the cells, and the frog's skin changes color.

BEFORE AND AFTER

Color changes in frogs can be dramatic. One tree frog pictured above is green, while the other one is brown. Scientists disagree about why this happens. Is it to match surroundings or due to temperature and humidity changes?

WARNING COLORS

Some species of amphibians have special glands in their skin that give off poisonous fluids. These creatures do not need to hide, but they do need to make sure predators realize they are dangerous. The majority of poisonous amphibians do this by displaying contrasting patterns of bright warning colors. Most predators instinctively leave such flashy creatures in peace.

SPOTTED SALAMANDER

This North American amphibian grows up to 8 inches (20.3 cm) long. Its yellow spots tell predators it has poisonous skin, allowing it to hunt without being disturbed.

CLASSIC COMBINATION

This poison-dart frog's skin makes it hard to miss. Yellow and black are one of nature's most common warnings, used by everything from snakes to wasps.

POISON-DART FROGS

There are more than 230 species of poison-dart frogs, each with a different color and pattern. Poison-dart frogs get their name from the way they are used by South American forest people. The poison is extracted and used to coat arrowheads and darts.

MOVEMENT

Amphibians move in a variety of ways. Most people know that frogs hop, but not many realize that toads walk and salamanders shimmy. All amphibians can swim. A few types of frogs can even glide.

The longest hop ever recorded was 17.5 feet (5.4 m) by a South African sharp-nosed frog.

HOPPING

Hopping is a very efficient way of moving. A single short burst of energy carries the body a long distance. Frogs are specially designed for this way of moving, with long back legs that stretch out suddenly to force the body into the air. Hopping is not the most accurate way of moving, but it is a great way to escape predators. Predators' eyes cannot easily follow the jerky movement.

SHIMMYING

Most long-bodied amphibians shimmy along. Salamanders, newts, and caecilians all move like this, twisting their bodies from side to side to propel themselves forward. Shimmying is almost identical to the way salamanders and newts swim. The only difference is that on land they lift their legs up off the ground. Unlike hopping, it is quite a slow way of moving.

SLENDER SALAMANDER

Newts and salamanders have relatively short legs and can only move slowly on land. Most non-poisonous species only come out at night, to avoid predators.

WALLACE'S TREE FROG

Some tree frogs escape danger by leaping into the air. As they fall, they spread out their webbed toes and fingers. The webbing works like a parachute to slow their fall. A few species, such as Wallace's tree frog, can actually glide, moving forward through the air as well as dropping down. Its large webbed feet act like a cross between wings and a parachute. By adjusting the position of its legs as it drops, it can even change direction in midair, aiming for broad-leafed plants to cushion its landing.

Wallace's tree frog lives in the tropical rain forests of Malaysia. It glides to escape danger or move between trees.

DOING THE WALK

One of the main differences between frogs and toads is the way they move. Unlike frogs, which hop everywhere, toads can hop or walk along. Toads' back legs are shorter than those of frogs, and this is what makes it possible for them to walk. Unlike newts and salamanders, toads keep their bodies straight as they move over the ground. However, like newts and salamanders, a toad moves its right front leg and back left leg forward at the same time. As these push the body forward, the other two legs are lifted off the ground.

NATTERJACK TOAD

Toads can move quite quickly, but most are still nocturnal to avoid predators and to keep from drying out. The natterjack toad is easily identified by the long stripe down its back.

PREY

All adult amphibians are carnivores. Most hunt small, slow creatures, but a few tackle bigger, speedier prey. Although amphibians are hunters, they are also often hunted themselves.

CARNIVORES

Although they might not look fierce, amphibians are killers. Most are active hunters, wandering under cover of darkness in search of prey. Most frogs, newts, and salamanders feed on slugs, insects, and worms. Toads prefer bigger prey when they can find it. A few species even eat small rodents, such as mice.

SLURP!

Frogs, toads, and some salamanders have sticky tongues to capture prey. Insects are hit from a distance and dragged into the amphibian's mouth.

CRUNCH!

Toads have wide mouths, enabling them to eat large prey. A toad may crush its victims with its jaws, but it does not chew them. All amphibians swallow their prey whole.

CANNIBALS

Amphibians are not picky eaters. If prey moves and is smaller than they are, they will try to catch it. Some amphibians even eat smaller members of their own species. Cannibalism is most common among amphibian young. Tadpoles of many species will attack each other when food is scarce.

RED SALAMANDER

Many amphibians have poisonous skin that makes them dangerous to eat. They advertise this with bright colors. A few nonpoisonous species, like the red salamander, copy these warning colors so that they are also left alone. The red salamander is unusual because it hunts other salamanders as well as small prey.

PREYED UPON

Most amphibians are quite slow-moving and small. As a result, they often fall prey to animals such as snakes. Many snakes, such as grass snakes, will even follow their prey into the water and hunt them there. Most amphibians avoid predators by hiding or being poisonous, but a few have other tactics. When it encounters a snake, the common toad inflates its body and stands upright to make itself look bigger.

TEXAS BLIND SALAMANDER

Many amphibians hunt by sight, but for some species this is not an option. The Texas blind salamander has no eyes, and even if it did, it would not be able to see anything. It lives in pools and rivers in underground caves. Living in total darkness, it finds prey by sensing pressure waves in the water. When prey move, they send ripples through the water around them, which the salamander senses.

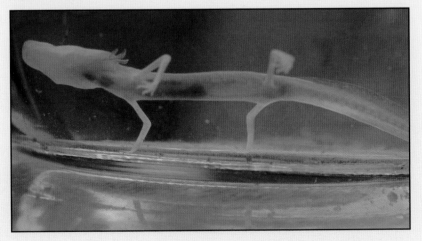

The Texas blind salamander takes oxygen from the water using feathery gills on the back of its head.

SNAKE FOOD

Newts and salamanders are the favorite prey among many snakes. Slow-moving and almost defenseless on land, they stand little chance of escape once they have been spotted.

COURTSHIP

Most amphibians need water to breed. In the tropics, they can breed all year. In other places, they usually gather in spring at ponds and other areas of fresh water.

TREE FROG

This tree frog has inflated its neck sac for calling. Different frog species make different noises. This helps females find a mate of their own kind.

ATTRACTING A MATE

Before breeding, amphibians have to find mates. Most male frogs and toads do this by calling. They inflate sacs under their throats or on the sides of their heads and force air over structures that vibrate, making noise. A frog's croak is a way of attracting a mate, although some make very different sounds. Male newts and salamanders grow frills or change color for the same reason.

SPRING PEEPER
This North American frog sings to attract a mate in early spring. Female spring peepers lay eggs on the stems of water plants.

EASTERN NEWT

As with many newts, North America's eastern newt has elaborate courtship behavior. The male (left) nudges his mate while twitching and fanning his tail.

BREEDING

The process of breeding almost always takes place in water. The female lays her eggs in the water, and the male drops his sperm on top to fertilize them. Male newts and salamanders guard their female until she has finished laying, chasing off other males that come too close. Male frogs and toads literally grab on to their mates and do not let go until the whole process is over. Sometimes several males try to grab the same female, with only the strongest succeeding in fertilizing the eggs.

GLASS FROGS

Male frogs and toads clasp their mates tightly by a process known as amplexus. The male wraps his front legs around his mate's neck or behind her front legs. Sometimes males hold on for days.

SPRINGTIME GATHERINGS

In temperate regions, frogs and toads gather in large numbers to breed in spring. This gives their tadpoles enough time to grow and become tiny frogs before the pond dries up or winter returns.

Mass spawnings help ensure that plenty of tadpoles survive. Predators such as birds are unable to eat all of the eggs, so enough will develop and hatch.

FERTILIZED EGGS

Once the eggs are fertilized, tiny tadpoles begin to grow inside them. The tadpoles feed on yolk inside their intestines. The jelly surrounding them acts as protection while they grow.

STRANGE BREEDERS

Most amphibians lay their eggs in water, but some have come up with different ways of breeding. Most of these lay fewer eggs, which they protect.

MALES HELPING OUT

Surprisingly, it is often male amphibians that look after eggs and young. Midwife toads mate on land, with the male fertilizing the eggs as the female lays them. The male then wraps the string of eggs around his legs and carries them until they hatch.

A REAL MOUTHFUL

A male Darwin's frog, from South America, gobbles up his tadpoles. The young then grow in his vocal sac. He spits them out three weeks later, after they have become tiny frogs.

CARING FATHER

The midwife toad, from western Europe, carries his mate's eggs for weeks, dipping them into water every so often to keep them wet. When they are ready to hatch, he lowers them into a pond.

POUCHES AND POCKETS

Some amphibians have special structures for carrying eggs. The female Surinam toad carries hers in pockets on her back. As she lays her eggs, her mate fertilizes them and pushes them into spongy tissue on her back. Her skin then grows around them, and they stay there until they are ready to hatch.

FOAM BREEDERS

In humid places, tree frogs lay their eggs in the open air. Elsewhere, the eggs need protection to keep from drying out. Some tree frogs make foam nests for their eggs above dried-up pools. The foam quickly hardens, forming a crust. When it rains, the crust dissolves, and the tadpoles fall into the water below.

MARSUPIAL FROG

The female of this South American species has a pouch on her back for carrying eggs. The male helps her push the fertilized eggs into the pouch, where they stay until they are ready to hatch. She then squeezes them out into water, using her feet.

TRUSTING LUCK

Most frogs and toads lay dozens of eggs in water and then leave. In tropical rain forests, eggs can be laid on land without risk of drying out. Some frogs take advantage of this by laying their eggs on tree leaves and other places above water, rather than in it. Here, the eggs are less likely to be eaten. When they hatch, the tadpoles simply wriggle out and drop into the water below.

Foam breeders make their nests from egg jelly, whipped up with their back feet.

LEAF NEST

Glass frogs live in the tropical rain forests and cloud forests of South and Central America. They lay their eggs on large leaves overhanging rivers and streams, where they are well out of the reach of most predators.

"TWO LIVES"

Most amphibians' bodies change shape as they grow. They hatch as tadpoles with gills, but as they get older they develop lungs and other adult features.

NEWLY HATCHED FROG TADPOLE

Frog and toad tadpoles have gills on the surface of their bodies when they hatch. Within a few weeks, the gills are covered by a pocket of skin.

FROG TADPOLE WITH LEGS

The first adult features that tadpoles grow are tiny back legs. These appear after about five weeks. Three weeks later, the front legs appear.

WATER-BORN

Almost all tadpoles start their lives in fresh water. When they hatch, they have feathery gills for breathing and long tails to help them swim. Most young tadpoles feed on algae, but as they grow they turn into little hunters. The majority of amphibians lay lots of eggs at once. This ensures that enough tadpoles will survive predators and become adults.

CHANGING SHAPE

As tadpoles grow, they change. This process is called metamorphosis. This is a Latin word that literally means "change formation." Frog and toad tadpoles start to grow little legs. The back legs grow first, followed by the front ones. When they are about 10 weeks old, tadpoles look like tiny adults with stubby tails. Over the next few weeks, their tails disappear.

FROGLET

Around 11 weeks after hatching, froglets emerge to live on land. They now have all their adult features but still have lots of growing to do.

26

SMOOTH NEWT LARVA AND ADULT

Salamander and newt larvae keep their feathery external gills until they become adults. Unlike frog and toad tadpoles, they grow their front legs first. Another difference is that they eat tiny animals rather than algae when they hatch.

COMING ONTO LAND

As tadpoles become miniature adults, they lose their gills and develop lungs. Most then leave the pools in which they hatched to find food on land.

Amphibians are the only vertebrates to have a life cycle like this. The word *amphibian* means to live both on land and in water. A few amphibians never leave water, and some caecilians give birth to live young, but they are rare exceptions.

AXOLOTL—THE ETERNAL NEWBORN

Many axolotls never go through metamorphosis. Instead, they keep their newborn body shape, complete with gills, and spend their lives in water. These axolotls are still able to breed once they have grown big enough. Not all axolotls stay in the water. Some do change shape and move onto land.

The axolotl lives wild in just a few lakes near Mexico City, although many are kept as pets.

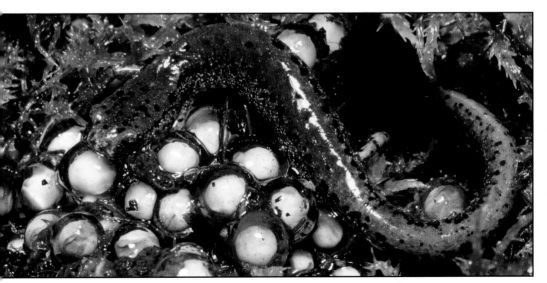

PARENTAL CARE

The four-toed salamander is unusual in that it mates and nests on land. It usually nests in mossy places or among fallen leaves so it is hidden from predators. Some four-toed females form communal nests where they take turns guarding each other's eggs.

SALAMANDERS AND CAECILIANS

Four short legs and a long finless tail make salamanders easy to recognize. With tiny eyes and no legs, caecilians look more like worms than amphibians.

AQUATIC SALAMANDERS

Most salamanders spend their adulthood on land, but a few never leave water. Mud puppies and most sirens have external gills, which they keep as adults. Other aquatic salamanders, such as the hellbender, have internal gills and folded skin to take oxygen from the water. The hellbender is the third largest species and can reach 29 inches (73.6 cm) in length.

MUD PUPPY

This North American aquatic salamander grows up to 13 inches (33 cm) long. It lives in rivers, lakes, and marshes. Mud puppies feed on other water creatures, including insect larvae and crayfish. They are usually nocturnal and hide away during the day.

CAECILIANS

Caecilians spend most of their time hidden under fallen leaves or in the soil of tropical rain forests. Their lifestyle means they are hardly ever seen by humans, and little is known about them. We do know that they are carnivorous and find most of their food by touch.

LESSER SIREN

This eel-like aquatic salamander lives in North America. It has no back legs and can grow to more than 2 feet (60 cm) long.

The largest caecilians grow to 5 feet (1.5 m) long, and some bear live young.

YELLOW-EYED SALAMANDER

The yellow-eyed salamander lives in the forests of North America. This species is most active after heavy rain. Like most other salamanders, it is mainly nocturnal.

LAND LOVERS

Some land salamanders look a bit like lizards, except for big, bulging eyes and smooth skin. Although common, land-living salamanders are rarely seen. Their small size makes them easy prey, so most only come out to feed after dark. Some salamanders mate on land, but most either lay their eggs or give birth to live young underwater. Once they have changed from their first juvenile form they stay as they are, unlike newts, which go through a second metamorphosis.

WARNING COLORS

The fire salamander lives in the forests of Europe, where it hunts by night for invertebrate prey. The large glands behind its eyes can squirt poison at attackers.

SLIMY SALAMANDER

Another North American salamander, this creature is named after the sticky mucus it secretes when threatened. Slimy salamanders lay their eggs on land. These hatch as tiny fully formed adults.

ARBOREAL SALAMANDER

This salamander is unusually good at climbing trees and has a prehensile tail. This means that it can wrap its tail around branches to get a firm grip.

NEWTS

ewts are similar to salamanders but have three different life stages. Adult newts spend more time in the water than most salamanders, despite the fact that they have lungs and breathe air.

This smooth newt is about to return to the water. It has already begun the change from eft to adult, although it has yet to grow its webbed tail fins. If it is a male, it will develop a frill on its back.

FROM LARVA TO EFT

All newts begin their lives in water. When they hatch, they have feathery gills and are known as larvae. They stay like this for a few months, then start to go through their first metamorphosis. As they change, their gills start to shrink, and lungs grow. Often, their color changes, too. Once their gills have gone, they leave the water. At this point, they are known as efts.

FROM EFT TO ADULT

An eft is a land-living juvenile newt. Most newts spend two or three years as efts, feeding on slugs, worms, and insects as they slowly grow toward adult size. Once they reach the size of adults, they begin to go through their second metamorphosis. Inside their bodies, the organs they will need to produce young start to grow. At that time, the efts return to the water. As they change into adults, most newts develop fins along their tails for swimming. Some change color, and the males of many species grow frills or crests on their backs.

NOCTURNAL FEEDER

Like salamanders, most newt efts feed at night to avoid predators. For this reason, although they are often quite common, newt efts are rarely seen. By day, they hide under logs, stones, or in thick vegetation.

COURTSHIP AND BREEDING

In spring, adult male newts start to search for a mate. Once a male finds a female, he begins his courtship. Different species have different courtship routines, but most involve the male spreading chemicals called pheromones toward the female with his tail. If the female accepts his advances, the male deposits a package of sperm, which the female picks up. She then leaves him and lays her fertilized eggs, usually one by one on the leaves of water plants.

GREAT CRESTED NEWT

This species lives throughout Europe. Adult male great crested newts like this one have long, jagged frills along their backs. They also have bright yellow bellies and large fins running along the top and bottom edges of their tails.

RED EFTS

This eft is the juvenile, land-living stage of North America's red-spotted newt. Its bright colors advertise the fact that it is poisonous, so most predators leave it alone. Red efts live on land for several years before they start to change into adults. As they change, their color becomes more dull, they grow tail fins, and they almost double their size.

Red efts are most common in moist wooded areas, where they feed on invertebrates.

ROUGH-SKINNED NEWT

This newt from western North America is poisonous and should not be touched. The land-living stage is actually an eft, but unlike most other efts, it is often seen wandering around in daylight. As the male newt matures, its skin becomes smooth, and it returns to the water to breed. Adult females also return to the water, although their skin remains lumpy.

TREE FROGS

Many frogs actually live in trees rather than ponds. Tree frogs have their own families—Hylidae, Hyperoliidae, and Rhacophoridae—and all are specially adapted for life in the forest.

WHY LIVE IN TREES?
Like all frogs, tree frogs are carnivores. In the tropics and subtropics, where tree frogs live, the vegetation is much thicker than in temperate regions. The frogs climb trees in search of food. In rain forests, hardly any light reaches the ground. Insects and other invertebrates are much more plentiful high up in the branches. Tree frogs are also better at escaping predators than their cousins on the ground, since they can hop away onto thin twigs or leaves.

GRAY TREE FROG

This North American tree frog lives as far north as southern Canada. It prefers damp forests and is more often heard than seen, emitting a whistle that lasts for about two seconds.

PACIFIC TREE FROG

The Pacific tree frog is found in parts of North America. Its striped "mask" makes it easy to identify, as do its long, slender legs and large, round toe pads.

RED-EYED TREE FROG

This species lives in Central America. Female red-eyed tree frogs lay their eggs on leaves overhanging rain-forest pools. When the eggs hatch, the tadpoles drop into the water.

POISON-DART FROGS

Poison-dart frogs resemble tree frogs but have their own family. These frogs from tropical South and Central America are among the most colorful animals on Earth. Though they are hardly ever more than 2 inches (5 cm) long, they stand out like jewels in the rain forest. Poison-dart frogs have very few natural predators, because the mucus on their skin is filled with nerve toxins.

Blue poison-dart frog

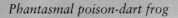

Phantasmal poison-dart frog

All poison-dart frogs are dangerous, but the golden poison-dart frog is the most deadly of all. The skin of just one of these tiny amphibians contains enough poison to kill more than 1,000 people.

Golden poison-dart frog

AMAZING FEET

Tree frogs can climb because their toes have suction pads that stick to leaves and bark. Most tree frogs are light, which also makes it easier for them to hold on.

YELLOW TREE FROG

Most tree frogs can walk as well as hop. Their long toes are not only sticky but can be wrapped around twigs.

MANY SPECIES

More than 1,340 species of tree frogs have been identified so far. Scientists think that there are probably many more yet to be discovered, since large areas of the frogs' rain-forest habitat are still unexplored.

LEAFY GREEN

Camouflage is important to most tree frogs. Their main enemies are tree-climbing mammals and snakes.

Of the 5,763 known species of amphibians, 4,532 are frogs. Frogs are found everywhere from tropical rain forests to deserts.

LIFE ON THE GROUND
Tree frogs make up nearly a third of all frogs. The rest live on the ground.
Like their tree-dwelling relatives, land-living frogs are active hunters that feed on invertebrates and other small creatures.

RED-LEGGED FROG
This species, common in western North America, is named after the red shading on its underside.

LEOPARD FROG
A widespread North American species, this frog hibernates in sheltered spots to avoid the worst of the winter.

FROG HABITATS
Frogs' skin loses a lot of water. In order to survive, frogs must live to either in wet, humid habitats or near fresh water. Even so, some frogs manage to live in deserts. They do this by waiting out the periods between rainfalls cocooned in waterproof underground capsules.

MASTER OF DISGUISE
The horned frog from Malaysia lives on the rain-forest floor. It has almost perfect camouflage. Its skin is the color and pattern of fallen leaves, while its body is ridged and pointed to mimic the leaves' shapes.

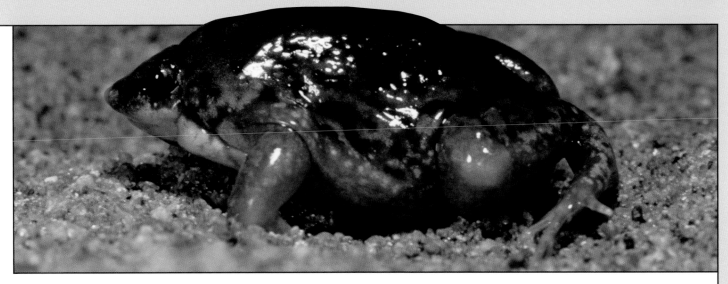

SPECIAL ADAPTATIONS

Some frogs have special physical adaptations to help them survive in their unusual habitats. The water-holding frog lives in Australia's deserts and emerges on the rare occasions when there is heavy rain. It spends the rest of the time in its watertight cocoon, as much as 3 feet (90 cm) underground. Like many burrowing frogs, it digs using its shovel-like feet. Once underground, it survives on water stored in its specially enlarged bladder.

DESERT DWELLER

Many desert frogs have rounded bodies to help prevent water loss. A rounded body is compact, and has less surface area through which water can be lost.

SHOVEL-NOSED BURROWING FROG

A pointed, flattened head helps this frog dig. Once the desert pools in which it breeds disappear, it is forced to head underground to keep from drying out. Like most other desert frogs, it retains a supply of water in its body.

THE TAILED FROG

Most adult frogs do not have tails. But the male members of one family, Ascaphidae, keep a small tail-like flap throughout their lives. Called tailed frogs, they are the closest living relatives to the first amphibians. Their eggs are unusually large and take longer to hatch than those of any other type of frog.

The Canadian tailed frog

TOADS

Frogs and toads are similar but have subtle differences. Frogs hop, while toads can hop and walk. Toads' skin is more dry than frogs' skin, enabling them to spend more time out of water.

OUT AND ABOUT
While frogs are most active during wet weather, toads can also come out to hunt when it is dry. Most toads are nocturnal to help them avoid predators, but occasionally they can be seen wandering around during daylight hours as well.

COMMON TOAD

This species is one of Europe's largest toads. It lays its eggs in long strings rather than clumps.

DRY NOT SLIMY
Although most toads have to return to the water to breed, they spend most of their adult lives on land. The secret to their success is their thick, dry skin. It is watertight and keeps them from losing water. Contrary to popular myth, touching a toad will not give you warts.

GOLDEN TOAD

The golden toad (below), from Costa Rica, is one of the world's rarest amphibians. Some scientists think that it may even be extinct, because a living one has not been seen since 1989.

FOWLER'S TOAD

This toad lives as far north as Ontario, Canada. During its breeding season, the male makes a long screaming sound to attract a mate.

TOAD FAMILIES

There are more than 500 known toad species, and these are grouped into five different families. By far the largest of these is Bufonidae, which contains more than 90 percent of all the world's toads. The other families, Pelobatidae, Pipidae, Discoglossidae, and Rhinophrynidae, include midwife, spadefoot, and clawed toads.

COUCH'S SPADEFOOT TOAD

This toad lives in the dry, open habitats of southwestern North America. It uses its spadelike feet to bury itself during droughts.

TREE TOADS

A few species of toads are able to climb trees. Like tree frogs, these tree toads have small suction pads on the ends of their toes. Despite their name, tree toads actually spend most of their time on the ground. They feed mainly on ants, which they hunt at night. Tree toads lay their strings of eggs in forest streams. The tadpoles are able to use their mouths like suction cups to cling onto rocks and underwater plants.

The marbled tree toad lives in tropical Asia.

SURINAM TOAD

This species carries its eggs in pockets on the skin of its back. Like its close relative, the African clawed toad, it spends most of its life in water and has sensitive toes to help it detect prey.

37

GIANTS

Most amphibians would fit in the palm of your hand, but a few are real monsters. The biggest amphibian is the Chinese giant salamander, which can grow up to 6 feet (1.8 m) long! It is closely related to North America's hellbender, which can reach 2.5 feet (75 cm).

PACIFIC GIANT SALAMANDER
This is the largest land-living salamander in North America, growing up to 14 inches (35.5 cm) long. The Pacific giant salamander lives along the west coast of the continent, from British Columbia, Canada, to northern California.

BIG TROUBLE
Giant amphibians can cause giant problems. In Australia, marine toads not native to the country have almost taken over. The toads were introduced from South America in 1935 and released to control beetle populations. Unfortunately, they ate many rare frogs and lizards as well. With no natural predators in their new home, their numbers increased at a great rate.

MARINE TOAD
With a head and body length of up to 10 inches (25 cm), this is the world's largest toad. It is also called the giant toad or cane toad. If attacked, glands in the skin produce a poisonous mucus, so most other animals leave it alone.

RECORD BREAKERS

The Goliath frog is the world's heaviest frog, but it is not the longest. That title goes to the North American bullfrog. With its legs stretched out, a big bullfrog can grow to 3 feet (90 cm) long.

Giant salamanders are even heavier than Goliath frogs. The Chinese giant salamander can weigh up to 143 pounds (64.4 kg). It lives in fast-flowing mountain streams, where it feeds on fish, turtles, frogs, invertebrates, and aquatic mammals. Its close relative, the Japanese giant salamander, has a similar lifestyle. It reaches 5 feet (1.5 m) long.

GIANT MONKEY FROG

This species is one of the world's biggest tree frogs. Females can have a head and body length of up to 4 inches (10 cm). The giant monkey frog's skin produces a very strong poison.

GOLIATH FROG

This giant lives in the Cameroon and Equatorial Guinea rivers in western Africa. It is the world's heaviest frog, yet its eggs and tadpoles are the same size as those of most other frogs. Nobody knows why it grows so big. Unlike most frogs, this one is silent, since it has no vocal sac.

Goliath frogs can weigh up to 8 pounds (3.6 kg).

SURVIVAL TACTICS

Amphibians have many enemies. Their small size makes them prey for a wide range of predators. To protect themselves, some have unusual defense techniques. Others are masters of survival in the world's toughest habitats.

ALL PUFFED UP

The common toad inflates its body and stands on tiptoe when it sees a snake. This tricks the snake into thinking the toad is larger and more powerful than it actually is, and the snake leaves it alone.

STAYING ALIVE

Life for most amphibians is a series of risks. Every time they leave their hiding place to search for food, they run the risk of becoming a meal themselves. Many amphibians are nocturnal to help them avoid predators, such as birds, for example, that sit in their nest at night. If they see a predator, some amphibians have defensive tactics that they put into action. Others rely on their camouflage, staying completely still in the hope that they will not be spotted. If that fails, most just try to make a run for it.

WARNING FLAGS

Not all poisonous amphibians wear their colors on their backs. Some are dull for camouflage on top but have bright patterns underneath, which they display if a predator shows too much interest. Many are unpleasant-tasting rather than deadly, but their colorful warnings have the same effect.

Yellow-bellied toads are poisonous. They lift up their bellies to show their warning colors.

A DESPERATE RESCUE

The instinct to protect young can be strong, even in amphibians. This male African bullfrog is saving his tadpoles from a drying puddle by digging a channel to a nearby pool. According to the photographer, the effort took the bullfrog five hours, but it was worth it. In the end, more than 1,000 tadpoles swam to safety.

COPING IN HARSH CLIMATES

It is not just predators that threaten the lives of amphibians. The weather also brings danger. Drought is a particular problem for these animals because many lose water readily through their skin. To avoid drying out, most desert amphibians take refuge underground and wait for the next rainfall.

WATER-HOLDING FROG

This species slows down its body processes to conserve energy through the long dry spells in its desert habitat.

LYING LOW

Plains spadefoot toads bury themselves after breeding and stocking up on food and water. They use their spadelike feet to dig down through the sand. This toad is having a last look around before burying itself completely.

AMPHIBIANS IN DANGER

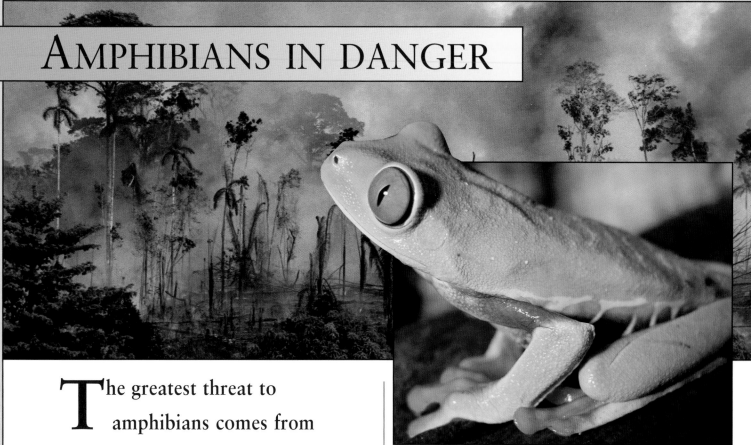

The greatest threat to amphibians comes from human activity. As we destroy natural habitats to make way for farmland, we destroy their homes. Other problems include hunting them for food and the pet trade.

RAIN-FOREST CLEARANCE
Tree frogs cannot live without trees. As the world's rain forests are cleared by loggers and farmers, tree frogs are killed or left with no homes. Scientists think that species are becoming extinct before they have even been discovered.

POLLUTED WETLANDS
Pollution from industry and other human activity often ends up in wild freshwater habitats. The amphibians that live there may be killed or develop problems that affect their breeding.

ON THE FRONT LINE
Many amphibian species live in very small areas of habitat. If those habitats go, then so do the creatures that depend on them. All around the world, natural habitats are being removed at an ever increasing rate to make room for the growing human population.

In order to save amphibians, we need to protect their habitats and make sure they always have somewhere to live. When saving habitats is not an option, the amphibians that live in them need to be captured and bred in captivity. That way, if their natural habitat is allowed to regrow in the future, they can be returned.

FROG SANCTUARY

Some amphibians are so rare that they may become extinct without help. Lake Titicaca giant frogs are being saved by a conservation program that breeds them in special ponds. The species is in danger because the wild frogs are hunted.

This giant was raised in captivity.

NOWHERE TO GO

Habitat loss is not just a problem in developing countries. The Pine Barrens tree frog lives in the western United States in certain swamps, bogs, and other endangered habitats. Its survival depends on these places being protected.

MYSTERIOUS DANGER

Scientists have noticed that many amphibians are becoming rare even though their habitats are undisturbed. The reason for this is not properly understood. Global warming and increased ultraviolet radiation from the sun, caused by the thinning ozone layer, are thought to be partly to blame. Other factors include disease, hunting, and increasing levels of dangerous chemicals in the air. These are all the result of human industry and energy production.

GOLDEN MANTELLA

This brightly colored little frog lives in the few remaining areas of rain forest in eastern Madagascar. Fortunately, it breeds well in captivity.

ANIMAL CLASSIFICATION

The animal kingdom can be split into two main groups, vertebrates (with a backbone) and invertebrates (without a backbone). From these two main groups, scientists classify, or sort, animals further based on their shared characteristics.

The six main groupings of animals, from the most general to the most specific, are: phylum, class, order, family, genus, and species. This system was created by Carolus Linnaeus.

To see how this system works, follow the example of how human beings are classified in the vertebrate group and how earthworms are classified in the invertebrate group.

ANIMAL KINGDOM

VERTEBRATE

PHYLUM: Chordata

CLASS: Mammals

ORDER: Primates

FAMILY: Hominids

GENUS: *Homo*

SPECIES: *sapiens*

INVERTEBRATE

PHYLUM: Annelida

CLASS: Oligochaeta

ORDER: Haplotaxida

FAMILY: Lumbricidae

GENUS: *Lumbricus*

SPECIES: *terrestris*

There are more than 30 groups of phyla. The nine most common are listed below along with their common name.

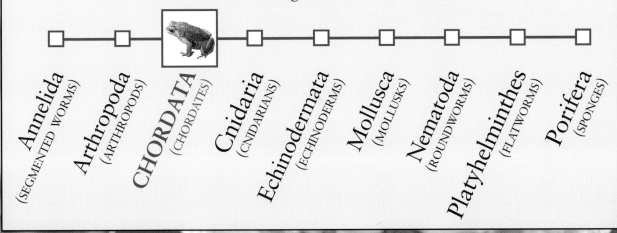

Annelida
(SEGMENTED WORMS)

Arthropoda
(ARTHROPODS)

CHORDATA
(CHORDATES)

Cnidaria
(CNIDARIANS)

Echinodermata
(ECHINODERMS)

Mollusca
(MOLLUSKS)

Nematoda
(ROUNDWORMS)

Platyhelminthes
(FLATWORMS)

Porifera
(SPONGES)

This book highlights animals from the Chordata phylum. Follow the example below to learn how scientists classify the *azureus*, or blue poison dart frog.

VERTEBRATE

PHYLUM: Chordata

CLASS: Amphibia

ORDER: Anura

FAMILY: Dendrobatidae

GENUS: *Dendrobates*

SPECIES: *azureus*

Blue poison dart frog
(azureus)

GLOSSARY

AMPLEXUS
When male frogs and toads cling to their mate to guard her while she lays eggs

AQUATIC
Living only or mostly in water

ARBOREAL
Living mainly in trees

CAMOUFLAGE
The disguising of an animal through shape, color, and pattern, to blend or merge with its surroundings

CARNIVORE
An animal that eats mainly other creatures, especially their flesh or meat

DROUGHT
A very long period of dry weather

EFT
A land-living juvenile newt

EXTERNAL
On the outside

EXTINCT
Died out; once a species has become extinct, it is gone forever

FRILL
A stiff flap that sticks out from an amphibian's neck or back

HABITAT
A particular type of environment where plants and animals live, such as a desert, mountainside, pond, or seashore

HIBERNATE
To go into a sleeplike state, usually during winter

HUMID
Damp; humid air is filled with water vapor

INTERNAL
On the inside

INTRODUCED
Brought by humans from another part of the world

INVERTEBRATE
An animal without a backbone or spinal cord; invertebrates include arachnids, insects, crustaceans, and mollusks

JUVENILE
Not yet adult

LARVA
An animal's young, immature body form before it becomes an adult; frog and toad larvae are called tadpoles

LATIN
The language used by ancient Romans; scientists use it to classify animals

MAMMAL
A warm-blooded vertebrate that feeds its young milk and has hair or fur

METAMORPHOSIS
A change in body shape and structure that most amphibians go though before they become adults

NATIVE
Originally from the place being talked about

NOCTURNAL
Active at night

OZONE LAYER
The layer of gases in the atmosphere that protects Earth from harmful sun rays

PHEROMONES
Chemicals made by an animal to attract a mate or otherwise affect the behavior of another animal of the same species

PIGMENTS
Colored chemicals in an animal's skin

PREHENSILE
Adapted for clinging or grasping, especially when referring to tails

REPTILE
A cold-blooded vertebrate with dry, scaly skin

TEMPERATE
Having to do with the areas immediately north and south of the tropical regions; the world's temperate regions generally have warm summers and cool winters

TROPICAL
Between the Tropic of Cancer and the Tropic of Capricorn on the world map; tropical regions are mostly warm and wet

TUBERCLES
Small bumps on an amphibian's skin

VERTEBRATE
An animal with a backbone and spinal cord; vertebrates include birds, mammals, reptiles, amphibians, and fish

FURTHER RESOURCES

AT THE LIBRARY

Badger, David P. *Frogs*. Stillwater, Minn.: Voyageur Press, 2000.

Clarke, Barry. *Amphibian*. New York: Dorling Kindersley, 2000.

Hofrichter, Robert. *Amphibians: The World of Frogs, Toads, Salamanders, and Newts*. Buffalo, N.Y.: Firefly Books, 2000.

Parsons, Harry. *The Nature of Frogs: Amphibians with Attitude*. New York: Greystone Books, 2000.

ON THE WEB
For more information on *amphibians,* use FactHound to track down Web sites related to this book.

1. Go to *www.facthound.com*
2. Type in a search word related to this book or this book ID: 0756512492
3. Click on the *Fetch It* button.

FactHound will find the best Web sites for you.

INDEX